Internet Millionaires Secrets

100 Internet Millionaires, How They Made Their Millions, Their Struggles, And Luck Breaks

DISCLAIMER

All the materials contained in this book are provided for educational and informational purposes only. No responsibility can be taken for any results or outcomes resulting from the use of this material.

While we have made every attempt to provide you with information that is both accurate and effective, the author does not assume any responsibility for the accuracy or use/misuse of this information.

The author has made every reasonable effort to be as accurate and complete as possible in the creation of this book and to ensure that the information provided is free from errors. However, the author/publisher assumes no responsibility for errors, omissions, or contrary interpretation of the subject matter herein and does not warrant or represent at any time that the contents within are accurate or current due to the rapidly changing nature of the Internet.

Any perceived slights of specific persons, peoples, or organizations are unintentional.

Table of Contents

Introduction

Life is all about evolution, accepting the changes it brings and making the most of it or disregarding everything and clinging to what we are comfortable with – that which we have come to know and accepted as life. Familiarity can be a friend that helps us blossom and an enemy that keeps us in fear and inaction.

The Internet is no different.

Like a quiet, unknown catastrophe straight out of a Stephen King novel, this mesh of wires and layered networks sneaked its way into our lives and embedded itself into every aspect of our day-to-day activity. Or is it the other way around?

The reaction from the masses was predictable. They either went for this new thing excitedly, or they just stared and wished it would go away.

For some early adopters of the Internet, it became a portal of wild opportunity that needed to be understood and ridden. The likes of Steve Jobs, Sergey Brin, and Bill Gates come to mind when you think of opportunists – while for others, this new shiny object was nothing but a phase that would run its course.

Well, here we are in 2020 with the power of hindsight vigorously active and the prospect of new frontiers ever before us. Here we are in a world that is being run on the back of these networks that has completely changed the way we live and do business.

The smartphone has replaced a lot of tech from previous generations and is an instrument that has become indispensable. This same Internet that was once used to exchange emails between students has become the lifeline for many millionaires. It became the silk road and uterus for many a brilliant idea that has revolutionized the world and turned the familiar on its head. Think back to the unveiling of the iPhone and how mobile shopping was introduced in the mix. These people – innovators and visionaries – saw opportunities where others did not. They ran ahead of the pack when others shuffled their feet in cold, brown sand.

They saw where the world was headed and decided they would get their first and maintain the lead. Since its inception, the Internet has served and supported anyone with the right idea and dogged determination to create wealth and keep a financially free lifestyle.

When Jack Ma had the idea for Alibaba, many told him it would not work. PCs were not a big thing in China; he saw and touched the first unit when he came to the US. Many tried to convince him that the Chinese market will never operate in a cashless system as the traders and business owners were used to physical currencies. Did that deter him? No. He went ahead and replicated that flea market then put it on a platform for the world to see. These days, Alibaba and its group of companies are responsible for fostering transactions coming from different parts of the world with China.

When Steve Jobs had the vision for the personal computer, very few could see it, and fewer still believed it. At every turn, he met with resistance. He met with resistance in his own company, and that saw him out on the street. Did that deter him? No. Didn't he go back out to start another computer company and a well-known animation company?

One of the questions on the mind of Internet users that come across in these stories of entrepreneurs is, why do some fail, and few succeed?

I can tell you right here and now without any need for facts and figures that one of the most crucial ingredients to being successful on the Internet is resilience. You expected me to say something deep and profound, right? I could have, but that would be fluff. Resilience is the stuff that makes these success stories; it is the fuel that kept them going regardless of hurdles and earth-shattering events. These entrepreneurs had their eyes on a goal and their desire for that intangible dream. And this indeed pulled them through and had their feet planted. A lack of resilience is the stuff of failure. Resilience builds stubborn patience under pressure; it takes a vision and amplifies its strength until the beholder is wholly consumed by it. The opposite of resilience is laziness. Laziness produces shoddy work and mediocrity. No successful Internet Millionaire was lazy. Life never gives the lazy a head start over those who are bent continuously and plowing behind LCD screens, farmlands, and thought spaces. It is always the resilient hard workers that reap bountiful harvests while the weak fall by the wayside.

Now, there is not an exact figure that tells us how many Internet Millionaires there are on the planet; in 2014 alone, Australia produced 43,500, while the US made 500,000. This is a sharp contrast to Nasdaq's reported 2,000 dotcom millionaires in 2008 and the global figure of 920,000 in 2014. According to the 2017 Global Wealth Report, there are currently 36 million millionaires in the world—with about half of that number being Internet Millionaires—and this figure is on the rise! This significant rise is 170% higher than the number collected in 2000.

What this book seeks to achieve is two-fold: to list 100 millionaires that gained their wealth from the Internet, and to summarize their net worth and what they did.

In carrying out research and compiling this list, I was careful to avoid the big names on the Internet as this does not help the little guy much or serve as inspiration. This compilation is aimed at inspiring the reader to act. And carry out your research and hopefully delve deep into the money-making opportunities that abound on the Internet. This list will comprise everyday people like you and I that had to sacrifice time, energy, and other valuables to hack the wealth code hidden between the networks and are currently living the best version of their lives. If financial freedom is something that interests you and reading about simple people that are relatable in this regard catches your fancy, then I invite you to go through these pages and suck up the wealth of information presented. Please note that the position of millionaires in each group does not directly reflect their level of wealth; a bit of suspense is good for everyone. I thought that listing the names chronologically in their order of wealth might be a little bit boring.

1 to 5 Million Dollar Club

1. Tiffany Pham

Background

A Harvard Business School and Yale University alumni, Tiffany, is a problem solver and a go-getter that is interested in connecting women, thereby creating a better world. She founded Mogul to empower and link up women, especially those in business.

Lucky Break

The creation of Mogul happened as a side project while Tiffany was still working her day job; she coded and created the framework at night, which paid off on launch with 1 million users registering on the platform. Currently, Mogul has about 18 million subscribers and has been named the 'Best Website for Finding Top Talent.' There is not an exact number, but Tiffany is estimated to be worth at least 2 million dollars. In addition, to be an entrepreneur and speaker, Tiffany has modeled for Naturalizer and authored books that have made the bestseller list.

2. Amra Olevic

Background

Amra is a popular Instagram celebrity, makeup artist, model, and blogger that has been on the up and up ever since she stepped on the scene. Amra is among the wealthiest celebrities on Instagram, and her followers are 5.5 million. This Montenegro born immigrated to the US when she was nine after spending time between Croatia and Bosnia. She is an ambassador for Bellami Clip and also runs her line of designer shoes and bags. In 2014 she collaborated with Anastasia to produce the Amrezy Palette. Amra is worth 2 million dollars and is secretive with details of her life.

3. Jack Bloomfield

Background

At just 12 years old, Jack Bloomfield began exploring the field of business. Now, as an entrepreneur in the e-commerce space, mentor, and speaker, the Australian is making strides and breaking boundaries.

Struggle & Breakthrough

The 16-year-old always speaks on how the educational system does not necessarily provide the tools needed for an entrepreneur to thrive, nor does it encourage people to dream and do beyond their peers.

His first business, Next Gifts had him pedaling pre-made, custom greeting cards; this first company served as an introduction into how the world of e-commerce and customer satisfaction works. At the time of researching for this book, he has three businesses in the retail and e-commerce space that have earned him 7 figures each. And that is not all it has given the young entrepreneur – he has met with the former Prime Minister, Malcolm Turnbull and has shared a stage with Tony Robbins and other motivational speakers. For Jack, learning is an enjoyable process that involves sharing what he has learned from those long nights binge-watching videos on YouTube in a bid to understand how e-commerce works, and this he does so well through his mentorship program. He is estimated to be worth 2 million dollars, and his influence has been steadily growing online and at school.

4. Chan Peng Joon

Background

Peng Joon was born on Friday, the 9th of November 1984, in Kuala Lumpur, Malaysia. He almost flunked school but managed to keep at it until graduation, at which point he branched off by creating a guide to World of Warcraft.

Lucky Break

He made $7 seven months after he launched the guide, and the feeling of making money from the comfort of his room spurred him to rinse and repeat the process. This feeling backed by experience, aided him to create subsequent materials like Farmville Secrets, Escape the 9-5, and Build A Money Machine: Make Money Online, which was his major break into the industry. Peng Joon's wealth is primarily because of the books he has put out, speaking events, and digital content he creates. He is estimated to be worth at least 5 million dollars. It was not easy for the author to amass all he has, but utilizing the World of Warcraft community worked in his favor, and a searing need to not stay broke propelled him forward.

5. Nick Shackleford

Background

Like some of the millionaires on this list, Nick is not the type that is too popular or shares a lot of personal information online, although his work speaks volumes. He is the Co-founder of Structured Social, which is a marketing/branding agency that has been crushing the competition and doing great numbers for their clients. A former soccer player that has taken his knowledge of teamwork and applied it to the field of digital marketing and rugged advertisement, Nick has almost done and seen it all. He has nearly $85 million in ad spend and has worked with over 150 brands B2C brands to provide world-class revenue for money spent. Nick's net worth is currently valued at 5 million dollars, and the year is looking good for him. His primary tool of the trade is Facebook ads, and he does well with scaling agencies and showing how to make the most of a budget.

6. Chase Dimond

Background

Chase is an internet marketer and Co-founder of Boundless Labs, a marketing agency obsessed with results and working with e-commerce brands. In his work with these brands, Chase has made 7 and 8 figures in annual revenue for his clients. And he has doubled their mailing list in the process. Since the creation of his company over the last few years, Chase marketing agency has driven close to 25 million dollars in revenue for the brands. These figures are estimated to rise as the year progresses. Chase is also an instructor on Foundr, where he teaches email marketing and scaling up your brand.

Struggle

Getting several rejections and experimenting a lot with different methods when cold calling clients has given Chase a unique approach to marketing that very few have the sensibility to handle. Currently, his net worth is estimated at 4 million dollars, and his clients include Original Grain, TUSHY, The Chive, and IBEX.

7. Michael Patton

Problem Solver

Every year, there is a high rate of problems that come up with the delivery of goods ordered online. E-commerce is booming, but there is always a gap between shopping and getting what you ordered. Unfortunately, many entrepreneurs are not living up to their end of the bargain. This is precisely what Michael has been trying to compensate for; sitting in front of the computer staring at excel sheets would either drive most people mad or birth ideas, but not Michael.

Background

A graduate of the University of Minnesota, Michael worked in finance for a while before stumbling on the idea to take users' shopping experience a step further; his model speeds up the delivery time while helping brands maintain a level of trustworthiness. With $14 million in funding already, Michael is estimated to be worth 5 million dollars.

8. Lia Winograd

Background

Lia is the co-founder of Pepper, a brand built to create bras for small-sized women. Pepper was launched in 2017 as a Kickstarter campaign with a goal of $10,000, but 10 hours into the drive, the goal was reached, and Lia and co-founder, Jaclyn Flu, were pleasantly surprised. A graduate of NYU, the entrepreneur, has said that being steeped in the school's climate gave her the resources and information needed to create the brand and get it on its feet. Pepper has been projected to make $6 million in revenue in 2020, and Lia is estimated to be worth at least 3 million dollars.

9. GRETTA VAN RIEL

Struggle

Gretta van Riel is not as popular as some of the people on our list, but she is among the fastest rising entrepreneurs to watch out for. When she was 22 and broke with only $24 to her name, she started SkinnyMe Tea or SMT for short. With SMT, Gretta did not have the slightest idea what she was doing, but she braved the storm of ignorance and ventured into the world of entrepreneurship. She has a course on Foundr that teaches brands how to scale and grow their business and has since shared a costly mistake she made with Skinny Me Tea by ordering a large quantity from China without taking time to follow the right channels that assured a refund when things went wrong. According to Gretta, that mistake taught her a valuable lesson that has aided her decisions from that point on.

Breakthrough

SMT exploded, and she struggled to meet up with demand; 11 million transactions in 5 years, happy customers, and a Shopify *Build a Business* award suggests that she did more than managing. The taste of success can be addictive, and this had Gretta venturing into her next business. *The 5th Watches* and *Drop Bottle*. As if to prove her previous success was not a fluke, Gretta raked in one million dollars in a single day with *The 5th Watches*. Most recently, Gretta shifted gears into Influencer Marketing with her platform *Hey Influencers,* which is built with linking and growing the relationship between influencers and brands, a bridge, if you will, that links start-ups with influencers that resonate with their message. The 29-year old's net worth is estimated to be at 5 million dollars and is currently one of the wealthiest entrepreneurs in Australia.

10. Laura Lee

Background

Laura is a YouTuber that runs two channels with a combined subscriber base of around 4.4 million. The views on her videos clock 600 million, and this directly translates into revenue for her. Born on the 1st of September 1988 in Alabama, Laura was a preschool teacher before working as a medical assistant for a dermatologist. Before her YouTube channel in 2013, Laura began posting pictures of her makeup looks on Instagram and saw a bit of traction, which propelled her to start a channel on YouTube dedicated to makeup tips, hacks, and tutorials. Laura has collaborated with well-known cosmetic brands to produce branded products and has endorsement deals that bring money to her account. Her net worth is estimated to be around $1.5 million now.

11. Allison Klein

Background

Allison is a teacher, entrepreneur, and founder of Rose and Rex, a toy company particularly interested in pushing imaginative play as an essential part of a child's development. Allison is on a mission to create awareness about the importance of imaginative play in the cognitive, emotional, physical, and social development of a child. Her eco-friendly puppets, handmade blocks, and assortments of toys make it easier to build lifelong skills through play.

Struggle

Some of the most significant obstacles Allison faced with creating the company was convincing people on the importance of interactive play and creating the right toys that carried the values she had in mind. Most of Allison's sales are generated online, and she is estimated to be worth 2 million dollars – the company is projected to make $3.5 million in 2020.

12. Saoud Khalifah

Background

Ever wondered if the reviews on Amazon are genuine or not? Saoud learned the hard way when he received a box filled dust-coated capsules after being convinced by the reviews on a nutritional product he was interested in buying. That was the end and beginning for Kuwaiti immigrant, as he started Fakespot almost immediately so that no one else would fall into the same situation he had. The site uses artificial intelligence to analyze a boatload of reviews then scans for inconsistencies that point towards bias and lies. Saoud has been featured on Forbes' 30 under 30 and is estimated to be worth 2 million dollars.

13. Nikalene Riddle

Problem Solver

Nikalene bridged the gap between finding recipes and building a community that supports proper dieting. The Aussie found herself losing weight fast right after having her baby, searched around for recipes that could help, but nothing turned up. Nikalene did the logical thing and started Skinnymixers to solve the problem. It started from a Facebook community that shared tips and cookbooks to this giant network of over 145,000 members. Nikalene has written 5 recipe books that have done well through her website and have traveled to several countries based on suggestions from the community. Her estimated net worth is 1.5 million dollars.

14. Rachel Pederson

Background

Calls herself the Queen of Social Media and for a good reason. The mother of three is knowledgeable on every aspect of social media and has done tremendously well for her clients and students. Rachel was born on the 1st of April 1989 in Minneapolis, Minnesota.

Struggle & Breakthrough

She dropped out of college and had to survive on welfare for a bit. In 2016, Rachel decided it would be all or nothing, took the plunge with her husband, bled, and sweated until the results they were looking for started to come. They had zero savings in their account, no backup plan, and no college degree to fall on when they started. Now Rachel has been featured on USA TODAY, Funnel Hacker TV, and the Daily Mail. Rachel's net worth is estimated at 3 million dollars.

15. Allen Brouwer

Background

Allen Brouwer is the co-founder of BestSelf Co, an e-commerce start-up selling journals and other products specifically created to boost effectiveness and productivity. Allen is also particularly good at growth hacking and distilling complex information into digestible and actionable points. He and his co-founder Cathryn Lavery started an e-commerce business, raised funds through a Kickstarter campaign that exceeded the goal – they got $322,000 in 24 days. They took this capital and grew the idea to an 8-figure business. Allen made the Forbes 30 under 30 list under retail and e-commerce and has been mentored by the likes of Tony Robbins, Russell Simons, and Tim Ferriss. Allen's net worth is estimated at 3 million dollars.

16. Joanna Griffiths

Problem Solver

Joanna is a woman on a mission to make women comfortable in their own skin and intimates, enter Knix, leak-proof underwear for women. Knix was started in 2013, and by 2015, Knix's 8-in1 Evolution Bra morphed into the most funded fashion project to ever cross

Kickstart. Currently, the brand sells an item every 10 seconds, and Joanna has to keep track of everything and ship almost half a million orders yearly. Now, thee are 37 employees working under her at the moment, but she is looking at expanding to 50 employees to keep up with her brand's growth. Joanna is estimated to be worth $3 million, and her brand is fighting the lingerie war with already established brands.

17. Deeanne Akerson

Background

Deeanne Akerson is the CEO of Kindred Bravely, a brand built to provide expectant and new mothers with nursing and luxury maternity wear. Deeanne is a mathematician and former teacher and has always enjoyed solving problems and manipulating numbers, although her journey as an entrepreneur and business owner did not kick-off until she became a mother herself. Her vision for Kindred Bravely is to make functional yet stylish and comfortable clothing for mothers, and two years after launching, it was named one of Shopify's fastest growing online retailers. Several recognitions, mentorship, and ringing the NYSE opening bell later, and Deeanne's brand is still going strong. Her net worth is estimated at 2 million dollars.

18. Chris Vaccarino

Problem Solver

Influencer marketing has been on the rise, and Chris is riding the wave; more people want to purchase, consume, or wear what their favorite celebrities endorse and use. Chris makes this connection happen with his brand Fanjoy, which is geared at building a bridge between the fans and their heroes. The idea is to help these heroes create custom merchandise that would improve the experience with their fans. Chris understands the current wave and the mentality guiding it, so instead of focusing on trying to sell to people, his interest is on building a social media following that would make Fanjoy become an extension of the customer's established lifestyle. Chris's net worth is 3 million dollars.

19. Wendy Nguyen

Background

Wendy is a fashion blogger and Instagram celebrity born in 1986 with a drive for fashion and teaching others to look good. A lot of information about Wendy is not available online, although it has been speculated that her net worth is 4 million dollars. She has been counted among the most successful fashion bloggers the world over and has the followers to back it up. Wendy's YouTube channel has about 600,000 subscribers with several hundred million views. She was born to a mid-level income family, and deciding to stay the course with fashion was not the easiest of decisions, especially as a graduate of Psychology from UC Berkeley.

20. Dave Lindenbaum

Background

Humorously called Dave Kombucha because of his top product offered through his website GetKombucha.com. Dave is an entrepreneur and marketer that has taken his business and that of others to as high as 8 figures. Little is known about Dave other than his love for Kombucha, recipes, benefits, and how to make them. His passion for kombucha tea and marketing strategy has placed his website among the best when it comes to Kombucha – this is all based on customer satisfaction. Dave's knowledge of SEO techniques, sales marketing, and copywriting, as well as understanding social media, has played a significant role in his success. He is estimated to be worth 2 million dollars and can be found wherever Kombucha is mentioned on the Internet.

21. Dana Derricks

Background

Dana is a serial entrepreneur, copywriter, and marketer that has helped a ton of businesses convert interest into clients. Dana gets excited by challenges facing businesses as it gives him time to figure out solutions; solutions mean more money for the business involved. He runs a channel on YouTube where he gives out information and points to tools that will help the budding entrepreneur. Dana has also written books that have done well, and also runs an e-commerce store that caters to his interest in animals. He is estimated to be worth 2 million dollars and is continually pushing the envelope of what is possible and achievable with the internet business model.

22. Sunny Lenarduzzi

Background

Sunny Lenarduzzi is a Vancouver, Canada YouTuber that is best known for her marketing tips, branding strategy, vlogs, and advice in her channel, SunnyLenarduzzi. Sunny is very much interested in leveraging the power of YouTube to help entrepreneurs scale their business and reach their audience. She has over a decade's worth of experience in social media strategy, video content creation, and communication. Her channel has garnered a large following, and the views on her videos are above 12 million; Forbes named her channel, the must-watch YouTube channel that will change your business. Sunny's net worth is estimated to be 1 million dollars, and in 2017, she was named one of 50 women entrepreneurs to follow by The Huffington Post.

23. Steve Hewitt

Background

Steve is the CEO of the fastest-growing sportswear brand in the UK Gymshark and has worked in the capacity of Managing Director and Management Consultant. Before his role at Gymshark, Steve attended the Manchester Metropolitan University, graduating with a BA in Business and Sport Management. He went on to become the Commercial Director at Reebok UK, then Managing Director at Tiger Turf. With Gymshark, the game changed slightly because most of the sales operation and marketing is done online, social media, email, and advertisements. Steve is conversant with the intertwining of sports, business, and the mode of communication prevalent in this generation. His net worth is estimated to be 3 million dollars.

24. Viki Odintcova

Background

Currently signed to Marvin Models based in Moscow, Russia, Viki Odintcova is an Instagram celebrity and model that has garnered the attention of many. Her pictures are provocative and mostly featured in adult magazines. She advertises products ranging from weight loss, underwear, fitness facilities, and branded clothing. Born on the 15th of November 1993, in Saint Petersburg, Russia, the model, and social media personality has featured on the covers of Sports Illustrated and Playboy, to name a few. A graduate of marketing, Viki's Instagram currently has 5.1 million followers. Her net worth is 1.5 million dollars as of the last evaluation.

25. Jaclyn Hill

Background

Jaclyn is a YouTube personality and entrepreneur with a large following on Instagram and YouTube. She is also known for her line of cosmetics and her lip gloss.

Success

One of Jaclyn's business ventures was her partnership with Becca Cosmetics to produce the Champagne Pop collection, which sold off within 20 minutes of its release in 2015. This sale of 25,000 units alone netted Jaclyn a hefty sum, and she later sold the company to Estee Lauder for $200 million in 2017. There is not an exact number of how much she makes from YouTube, but it is safe to assume it is high when compared to how much other YouTube stars are making. The Photography graduate is estimated to be worth around 3 million dollars.

26. Kimberly Lewis

Struggle

Kimberly is the Co-founder of Curlmix, a natural hair product blend made to cater to the woman with curls. The company has been evaluated to be worth $12 million at the time of this publication, but the journey was not smooth for Kimberly and partner, who is also her husband.

Lucky Break

The two have been on Shark Tank to pitch their idea and got funding for their products; from the $1.4 million the duo got from the likes of Backstage Capital, the duo has taken Curlmix and generated over $7 million in 2019. Kimberly has spoken about how much time and effort goes into creating each product, especially their flaxseed gel, that seems to be one of their customer's favorite. Kimberly is estimated to be worth 4 million dollars and is set to put more effort into marketing online.

27. Jessica Stein

Background

Jessica is a travel blogger and Instagram personality that has been to over 27 countries. Her Instagram has 2.3 million followers, and her fan engagement goes from 77,000 to

100,000. She started with her blog named Tuula, which is Finnish for a word in 2010 and still maintains it. Born on the 20th of June 1984 in Germany but moved to Australia, Jessica has worked with brands like Land Rover and VitaminX, which cemented her stand as a blogger that is more than a pretty face. She is estimated to be worth 1 million dollars.

28. Emma Chamberlain

Background

Emma is an American YouTuber born on the 22nd of May 2001, who won the 2018 *Streamy Award* for Breakout Creator. Chamberlain grew up in a working-class family near San Francisco, California, and her parents got divorced when she was 5 years old. As a young kid, Chamberlain had a strong outgoing personality, which she came to realize she would want to use in her career one day. Chamberlain started making videos with friends and learning how to edit them; her father is a photographer and artist. With 8 million subscribers on YouTube and a similar number on Instagram, Emma is currently estimated to be worth 3 million dollars.

29. Mindy McKnight

Background

Mindy McKnight is an American YouTuber born on the 24th of June 1979 in Utah, United States. Her net worth is currently estimated to be 3 million dollars, and she was named among the Top 25 Woman of YouTube.

Success

Her YouTube channel has a large following, and her idea for Cute Girls Hairstyles came about in 2001 when she was tired reworking the same old hairstyle for her 18-month-old twin daughters – but she didn't put it out for the public until October of 2008. Mindy is the founder of the Cute Girls Hairstyles YouTube channel and creates hair tutorial videos with the assistance of her family. Mindy's twin daughters have gone ahead in their mother's footsteps by establishing themselves as YouTube stars.

30. Meredith Foster

Background

Meredith is a YouTube personality known primarily for her self-titled channel. Meredith was born on the 5th of November 1995 and posts lifestyle vlogs, fashion tips, and beauty tutorials to her over 4 million subscribers. Meredith has also made appearances on TV shows, and this has contributed to her fame and fortune. Very little personal information is in circulation about Meredith because she wants it that way, although her net worth is estimated at around 1.5 million dollars.

31. Eva Marisol Gutowski

Background

Born on the 29th of July 1994 in Brea, California, Eva Marisol Gutowski is a YouTuber, actress, author with a net worth of 4 million dollars. Her videos are in the areas of fashion, beauty, vlogs, makeup tutorials, and comedy. Her music videos also make an appearance sometimes. Eva comes from a humble background; her mother lost her job, and the family of four had to live in an apartment. Her first videos were meant for her friends, but once her channel started growing unexpectedly, she quit her job to face her channel full time. Eva graduated with a degree in Journalism from California State University and has appeared in a commercial for Chevrolet.

32. Ashley Zahabian

Background

Ashley is a keynote speaker, entrepreneur, YouTuber, and author that has shared the stage with some of the biggest names in the industry. By 21, Ashley had worked with Grant Cardone, Eric Thomas, and Gary Vaynerchuk and addressed more than 2 million people.

Born in Paramus, New Jersey, the 25-year-old studied and thoroughly understood the art form that is called public speaking, then used the power of social media to reach out to people she could not have met otherwise. She is estimated to be worth 2 million dollars at the time of this publication and has been featured on Forbes and The Huffington Post.

33. Patty Delgado

Struggle

Patty Delgado, 27, is the founder of Hija de tu Madre, a company based in Los Angeles that she started with $500 in savings stitched together from doing several odd jobs. Her first inspiration and piece came about when she sewed a patch bearing the revered image of the Virgin of Guadalupe onto a denim jacket.

Breakthrough

Patty's brand primarily handles sales through the website and has sold to more than 20 countries. She has not received any external funding and expects to make $2 million in revenue in 2020. Patty's products include bilingual planners, jackets, and jewelry, and her obsession with selling began since childhood when she would sell pencils and Tic Tac mints to classmates. Patty's net worth is estimated to be 4 million dollars.

34. Daniel Kane

Problem Solver

Daniel is a wallet salesman. A proud wallet salesman. His story is one unlike that of many entrepreneurs: from a young age, Daniel fell in love with making money. He would charge his friends for service you would hardly think to charge for. As he grew, he turned his attention towards e-commerce to sell retrofit Rock Band drum kits on forums and anywhere really on the Internet.

Success

His current obsession came about from the annoying bulge in his pockets when a wallet is involved. It annoyed him enough that he created a solution in the form of The Ridge Wallet, which is slim and easy to carry wallet designed to not get in the way. Daniel is estimated to be worth 3 million dollars, and the father-son found venture is doing well in the 8-figures department.

35. Dan Henry

Background

Dan is an internet marketer and founder of
GetClients. He has experience with the world

of social media marketing and creating content that delivers results; Dan has helped agencies scale and ran Facebook ad campaigns that brought in massive revenue. He used to be broke and trudged through life until he realized he could do so much more. He transitioned from running a club and holding down a brick and mortar business to being an internet authority. He has several courses that teach entrepreneurs how to grow their business, get leads, and run Facebook ads.

Success

Dan is a heavy user of ClickFunnels as opposed to the traditional use of a website, although he encourages his clients to get one. He recently published a book titled Digital Millionaire Secrets, where he outlines all his struggles and the path to being financially stable. His net worth is $5 million.

36. Ben Malol

Struggle

Ben is one of the leading Facebook Internet marketers in the world and has generated quite a handsome profit from running ads for clients and his e-commerce store. Recently, he has veered in a different direction with a heavy concentration on Bitcoin technology and how it can be leveraged in the coming revolution.

Breakthrough

Life was not easy for Ben, moving to Israel with his mother and sister when he was 9 and constantly moving afterward did not give him a stable life, but he made good use of this adversity. This came in handy when he met up with his partner in Israel to pursue social media marketing and e-commerce. He is estimated to be worth 5 million dollars at the time of this research.

37. Caleb Maddix

Background

It has been said that a rolling stone gathers no moss; this statement can be applied to Caleb. When he was 12 years old, Caleb authored his first book *Keys to Success for Kids* and has been very vocal about making his first million by the time he hit 16. Now 17, and estimated to be worth 5 million dollars, Caleb has shared the stage with Gary Vaynerchuk and started Apex For Kids. This on-demand video platform provides video content that entertains and educates children. Caleb has expressed how much he desires a new educational system that takes into account the Internet and how it can be leveraged for kids.

38. Brooklyn McKnight

Background

Born on the 31st of December 1999, Brooklyn is the daughter of YouTube star Mindy McKnight and the twin sister of Bailey

McKnight. Brooklyn and her sister first got noticed through their mother's channel before taking the plunge to pursue the social media lifestyle her mother keeps. The sisters run a channel together where they post beauty tips, hacks, fashion videos, and lifestyle vlogs. Brooklyn is rated among the wealthiest people in Utah and has over 6 million subscribers on her channel. Currently, her estimated worth is around 5 million dollars and may rise in the coming years.

39. Connor Blakley

Problem Solver

You have ever wondered how to reach Generation Z with your marketing? Connor has cracked the code and has a long line of clients to prove it; Hasbro, Microsoft, PepsiCo, Sprint, and NPD, to name a few. From a young age, Connor got bitten by the entrepreneurial bug and never stopped moving in line with his passion.

Success

From selling rocks to neighbors, starting a homework-selling network then starting a social media agency at 14, Connor has tried a lot in a short time. As an entrepreneur, speaker, and marketer, Connor has leveraged social media platforms to reach out to the rising generation and create an impact as he goes; he runs YouthLogic, an internet marketing firm explicitly aimed at the Generation Z. He is estimated to be worth at least 3 million dollars. Connor has worked with Jay Abraham, Daymond John, and Joe Polish.

40. Lindon Gao

Problem Solver

Necessity, they say, is the mother of invention. This is the story underpinning Lindon's drive to create an efficient payment system that does not waste time and is reliable. Along with his partners, Lin went on in January 2019 to create the first AI powered shopping cart; this method of payment is set to overthrow the current checkout methods used by stores and is being tried by Canadian grocery store Sobey's. Lindon has already raised $13 million in funding and is seeing more interested investors. Currently, Lin is worth 3 million dollars, and he is listed on Forbes 30 under 30.

41. Chandler Bolt

Problem Solver

Chandler decided he was going to drop out of college and make money instead! The itch to branch out of monotony brought on by classroom schedule had been enough, and he yearned to see what a full-time devotion to an unconventional business would yield. This was all in 2013, and by 2015, he had a million dollars! How did he do it, you ask? He self-published books that were answers to the needs of people; a book on time management was his first stab at the industry. The first month after publishing had him raking in almost $7,000 without so much as supervision on his end. Self-publishing on digital platforms is the mantra Chandler propagates, and he has an entire system and testimonial to back it up. The 25-year-old is currently worth 3 million dollars, and he expects to keep growing and scaling his business.

42. Taylor Pearson

Drive

Taylor is a man on a mission and gives off a vibe akin to Tim Ferriss. An author, entrepreneur, and life hack coach that uses the Internet as his platform and the stage as his rallying point, Taylor has influenced a lot of people to change the way they approach work in the society. As an avid traveler and observer,

Taylor has seen where the world is going, and he penned it down in his bestselling book *The End of Jobs,* which further pushed his reach and solidified his place as an authority in the field. Taylor is estimated to be worth at least 3 million dollars; the visionary is passionate about seeing a world where everyone works to their full capacity and attains fulfillment.

43. Danielle Bernstein

Background

Danielle Bernstein is an Instagram personality popularly known under the name WeWoreWhat. Apart from Instagram's fame, Danielle also runs her independent fashion blog and online store. Her store carries bags, clothes, and shoes, all of which are sold through her website.

Success

Interestingly, Danielle took a path down affiliate marketing avenue and had since been selling through Moda Operandi, Stella McCartney, and Miu Miu. Her account has over 2.5 million followers, and more are being added daily. Before fame and fortune, Danielle went to the University of Wisconsin-Madison but later transferred to the Fashion Institute in New York. She came from a modest family and got her to start writing fashion blogs. Danielle is managed by Next Models, and her rates range from $5,00 - $25,000/Instagram post. She has worked with big agencies like Avion Tequila, Fiji water, and Virgin Hotels and is estimated to be worth 4 million dollars.

6 to 10 Million Dollar Club

44. Gabriel Zamora

Rise and Rise

Gabriel is a fast-rising YouTube star with a cult following that reaches more than 850,000 subscribers. The strange thing is that Gabriel accomplished all this within 5 years of his initial post; his first upload happened in April of 2014. He quickly built up his audience and a solid fan base that support and consume the content he puts out. Before fame and endorsement deals, the college dropout experimented with makeup as a teenager and was recruited by Lilli Ghalichi while he was in school in Texas. He is the first male artist to sign with Michelle Phan's beauty community, Ipsy. He also partnered with makeup brand MAC to produce a line of lipstick and is estimated to be worth 10 million dollars.

45. Billy Gene Shaw

Background

Also known as Billy Gene Is Marketing, is an Internet marketer who sells courses and grows businesses for clients. Shaw, who is currently 31, graduated from the University of San Diego in 2009 and started Rethink and Relive LLC in 2011 geared towards crafting online courses that helped people break addictions. He had stated that he lost a client that was paying him $25,000 a month, and that taught him a huge marketing lesson that served as a boost for him and his business. His net worth is 9 million dollars, and his approach to marketing sets him apart from the competition; he does not pretend to be anything other than himself.

Struggle

His path to becoming the CEO of a 7-figure business had him cold calling clients – about a hundred daily – for an online school which gave him a taste of rejection and a measure of success. Facebook ads served as the opening door for Billy Gene, and this led him to pursue mastery and to offer his services to other businesses. His courses have him sharing all he has learned from running his ad agency as well as teaching effective ways to maximize and grow a business.

46. Zoe Sugg

Breakthrough

Zoe is an English writer, YouTuber, and entrepreneur known for her videos, blog, and young-adult novels. Zoe Elizabeth Sugg's source of income includes books she has authored, YouTube videos, and beauty products she has released. Zoe runs two channels on YouTube and has over 15 million subscribers combined. In 2014, Zoe released her debut novel Girl Online, setting a record for the highest first-week sales raked in by a debut author.

Background

Born in Wiltshire before moving to Brighton, Zoe started her YouTube channel out of boredom, but then it grew to her astonishment. She is estimated to be worth 6 million dollars at the time of this publishing.

47. Jimmy Donaldson

Background

Popularly known as MrBeast, Jimmy is a YouTube sensation that has made quite the name for himself by giving away money for social causes; he has given to homeless and total strangers. Donaldson's money primarily comes from endorsement deals than AdSense – Quid and Honey are two companies that support high traffic channels. However, it is the number of subscribers and views that affect how much money one gets from endorsements.

Philanthropy

On this matter, Jimmy does not say much other than the fact that his parents are not wealthy, but everything comes from YouTube. It is quite clear that giving out money to random people on the Internet and the street can be seen as a philanthropic act, and skeptics choose to see it as a marketing tactic designed to fuel Jimmy's popularity and bank account. He is estimated to be worth 6 million dollars.

48. Kristen Leanne

Path

Kristen is a well-known face in the cruelty-free beauty product space and has a large following on YouTube and Instagram. Together with her ex-husband Ryan Morgan, the duo created the brand Arctic Fox and encouraged viewers to use their products as an alternative to others that are not as concerned about the environment and animals. She is currently estimated to be worth 10 million dollars and had partnered with several media outlets like Collective Digital Studio to promote her products and create awareness.

Background

Kristen is 31 years old and was born in San Diego, California, and is known for her glittery presentation, tattoos, and bright colors. Finding a niche that worked well with her passions was an issue in the beginning, but experimenting with different styles brought her artistry to the fore and grew her social media following.

49. Robert Roizen

Background

Robert is the Co-founder of Feedonomics, a company founded by him and his brother to help retailers get listed across the web. Robert was listed on the Forbes 30 under 30 and had been doing a lot for businesses to gain traction and visibility on the Internet. His company charges a monthly subscription fee and has projected an income of $30 million in 2020.

Problem Solver

Before his work with Feedonomics, Robert worked at an advertising agency where he handled product optimization for retailers but got frustrated by the whole process and the limitations of the platforms available. Robert set out to solve this problem that existed in the data of so many retailers; he would know after handling a large chunk of data from so many retailers. Initially, Feedonomics was funded by Robert and his brother because not many venture companies would back them. Now, Robert is estimated to be worth 6 million dollars.

50. Adi Halevy

Persistence

How do you go from being a start-up with nothing to a thriving business? Adi has the answer; as CEO and Co-founder of Teami Blends, a natural tea company, and no prior marketing experience, she did the almost impossible. Adi never went to college; neither did she possess the quick mind of an entrepreneur, but she took what she had – a rugged determination to learn – and applied herself until success came her way. Her customer base is estimated at 200,000, and her rise has not slowed down one bit. Her estimated net worth is 6 million dollars, and she has been a lifestyle sensation across the US and abroad.

51. Tati Westbrook

Background

Tati is an influencer, entrepreneur, makeup artist, and YouTube personality with almost 1.2 billion views and over 10 million subscribers on her channel. Born on the 14th of February 1982, in Seattle, Washington, Tati started working as a makeup artist and image consultant.

Success Path

She tried her hand at acting, making appearances on episodes of the TV series Greek, before heading off to Twitter and YouTube in 2010. Apart from making videos, Tati also has a beauty brand *Halo Cosmetics Inc* that sells vitamins and promotes good health and well-being. She is currently estimated to be worth 6 million dollars and has made appearances as a beauty consultant on live shows.

52. Ben Francis

Background

Ben is a YouTuber, fitness expert, and entrepreneur from the UK. He is the Co-founder and Chief Brand Officer of Gymshark, a sportswear brand that is on the high rise. Ben was born on the 6th of June 1992, in England, and went to Aston University to study Business and Management. But he never did graduate.

Struggle

Ben built iPhone applications and websites that pushed whatever business he had at the time; 2 of the apps he created were geared towards fitness, and he tried his hand at building a social media website that didn't entirely take off.

Breakthrough

He started Gymshark out of his parents' garage in 2012 while selling pizza at night to fund his dream. Ben was only 19 at the time and could not have guessed that the company would blow up the way it did. He has videos on YouTube, showing how he went about creating Gymshark. In 2018, Gymshark made more than $120 million in sales revenue, and Ben is estimated to be worth 10 million dollars.

53. Dimitris Skiadas

Background

Dimitris is the guy e-commerce owners and fashion brands contact when they need to scale up or understand why their conversions are so low. He has been in the business for almost a decade and has aided over 50 Shopify store owners to understand Google, YouTube, Facebook, and to gauge their numbers accurately. Dimitris has worked with the biggest names in Greece and has clients the world over. Marketing and tweaking conversions are his primary weapon of choice. Dimitris is estimated to be worth 7 million dollars at the time of this publication. A master of Google Analytics, Dimitris teaches and inspires other entrepreneurs to hit the same 2 commas he has consistently hit with his business.

54. Joey Petracca

Problem Solver

Joey is the CEO and COO of Chicory, a company that is providing a platform that easily connects you to recipes online; it goes further than that by being a one-stop solution for e-commerce and advertising needs of brands and individuals. Joey has been listed on Forbes 30 under 30, and since the start of the company in 2013, he and his partner have facilitated millions of dollars worth of transactions. It is estimated that the company will cross the $25 million threshold in 2020. Information on Joey is scarce on the Internet, but he is estimated to be worth 9 million dollars.

55. Yuni Sameshima

Background

Yuni Sameshima is the Co-Founder and CEO of Chicory, a technology company based in New York that makes finding recipes easy and shoppable by employing artificial intelligence. The company, under Yuni and co-founder's watchful gaze, has grown to reach over 70 million viewers monthly since its inception in 2013.

Growth

Before starting Chicory, Yumi worked in the venture and food niche at Chobani. The 29-year-old graduate of Colgate University is estimated to be worth 7 million dollars. Yuni has spoken at several events and is known to be vocal about the direction e-commerce is headed in, and the role Chicory is playing in that movement.

56. James Charles

Background

Born on the 23rd of May 1999, in Bethlehem, New York, James made history when he became the first male ambassador for CoverGirl cosmetics. He is best known as a makeup artist, social media personality, and model; early on, his parents supported him by letting him convert their basement into a makeup studio.

Path

Initially, James started as a hairdresser before switching into makeup then started a YouTube channel in 2016. His channel has over 15 million subscribers and has over 1 billion views. Apart from income from social media and endorsements, James also sells Apparels. He is estimated to be worth 10 million dollars.

57. Hector Espinoza

Background

Hector is the co-founder of Multiplied, a marketing agency focused on digital marketing, public relations, and design, but have taken a turn into innovative blockchain projects geared at scaling marketing hurdles. Clients include Gods Unchained, Ampleforth, Celer Network, Elixxir, and Skale Labs. Before founding Multiplied, Hector worked as a digital marketing strategist for brands like Chick-Fil-A, St. Jude Children's Research Hospital, and more. With Multiplied, Hector has initiated, executed, and guided research, digital marketing campaigns that have gone viral, created valuable content, and proffered intelligent business solutions.

He is a diverse talent with specialties in several marketing categories that include growth hacking and marketing strategy. Hector is estimated to be worth at least 10 million dollars and is working tirelessly behind the scenes of blockchain technology.

58. Joel Brown

Beginning

An Aussie with addiction for success, Joel Brown started from small beginnings on Twitter before he took on other social media platforms. He started Addicted2success.com as an outlet for quotes and inspirational materials for budding entrepreneurs.

Success

After adding AdSense to his site, Joel began to see considerable revenue that rivaled his full-time job; brokers started making offers to the tune of $600,000 for his blog, but Joel refused to sell. Joel has sold over $2 million worth of products on his blog and is estimated to be worth 10 million dollars at the time of this publication. He has repeatedly stated how hard it was for him to grow his audience, but his love and addiction to success kept him going.

59. Jeremy Cai

Problem Solver

Jeremy is the founder of Italic, an online retailer that sells luxury goods without the high-ticket prices or brand names. The company went in a different direction by designing its own products then have brand name manufacturers make these items. In November, Italic raised $13 million in funding and moved with growth in its infrastructure. Jeremy is a college dropout, a Thiel Fellow, then founded Fountain, an online platform that helps companies find and recruit professionals. Jeremy has also invested in start-ups. His estimated net worth is 7 million dollars.

11 to 20 Million Dollar Club

60. Alex Morton

Background

Born on the 21st of October 1989, in Houston, Texas, Alex hit 6-figure income before he turned 21, and that only spurred him to do more. A graduate of Communications from Arizona State University, where he also obtained an Arizona Real Estate License and worked part-time leasing and selling off condos.

Success

Alex saw a measure of success as a real estate agent, but in 2011 things changed when he was introduced to network marketing for a health and wellness brand. This became his turn around when he became the youngest member in the company to hit the 1-million-dollar mark. Apart from his network marketing pursuits, Alex is also interested in giving back to the community and help raise others like him. He is estimated to be worth at least 20 million dollars now.

61. Juvan Langford

Mission

Having worked with clientele from Fortune 500 CEOs to professional sports clients, Juvan is known for his delivery, ability to inspire and equip people to be the absolute best version of themselves. By leveraging YouTube with his vlogs when he is not speaking on stages, Juvan has reached more people and changed lives than he would care to count.

Background

The 31-year-old had every disadvantage growing up, from living in a bad neighborhood to fighting for survival in a drug-infested climate, but he did not let any of that deter him. He is currently worth 11 million dollars as of the last evaluation.

62. Amanda Goldman-Petri

Background

A survivor of teen pregnancy, abuse, and near death, Amanda Goldman-Petri sells a non-hustling mentality; she teaches the novel concept of working smarter rather than harder. She runs Marketlikeanerd.com and has generated over 6 figures in the first 90 days after launch. As an Internet marketer that is reshaping workflow and approach in marketing, she has seen incredible results,

Amanda has been featured on major media outlets such as Fast Company, ABC, NBC, The Huffington Post, Small Business FOX, Trendsetters, CBSWorth. Currently, her net worth is 13 million dollars, Amanda helps businesses double their earnings without working harder.

63. Rand Fishkin

Struggle

Rand Fishkin's story is one we can somewhat relate to easily. A broke 25-year-old with a $500,000 credit card debt climbed the financial ladder and broke through barriers. It sounds like a scene straight out of a Hollywood movie, but this was Rand's situation. When he was 22, Rand dropped out of college and partnered with his mother to grow their business. This business had them placing ads in the Yellow Pages on behalf of businesses. It was slow at first, but then transitioned into making websites when the Internet began to grow in popularity; this was mainly because Rand had the foresight to pursue this new tool as businesses were transitioning.

Success

Their business grew from 2001 to 2004 to include conferences, contractors, office space, and a large debt. Around 2005, Moz began looking into SEO specifically to cater to the needs of his clients, which led him to create MOZ. The 40-year-old author, entrepreneur, and blogger is currently estimated to worth 12 million dollars, and projections predict this number will only shoot up in 2020.

64. Sean McLoughlin

Background

Born on the 7th of February 1990, Sean popularly known on YouTube as Jacksepticeye is a social media personality with a large following. He is best known for his vlogs and comedy series. Sean has described his videos as an assault on the senses and goes on to call himself the most energetic video game commentator on YouTube. Sean joined YouTube in 2007 but did not start uploading content until 2012 with the uploads of video games.

Success

In 2012, PewDiePie mentioned him on one of his videos, which led to Sean's explosive success. Currently, Sean's channel has over 12 billion views and around 23 million subscribers. The Irishman has close ties to fellow YouTubers, PewDiePie, and is a part of his network. He is estimated to be worth 16 million dollars, and this is money gotten mostly from his many endorsement deals and YouTube's monetary programs. Sean is also a comedian; his comedy tour, *How Did We Get Here,* helped with his popularity and the offers he got afterward.

65. Logan Paul

Background

Logan was born on the 1st of April 1995, in Westlake, Ohio. He was only 10 years old when he first started creating videos for Zoosh. As is typical with most kids, Paul got heavily involved in sports while in high school and entered wrestling competitions. He got into YouTube in its early days and put in a lot of creative working hours so much so that he had a pretty solid following by the time he graduated from high school. He went on to Ohio University but opted to drop out in 2014 in favor of pursuing a career in social media.

Success

His first big break came from Vine, which put him in the spotlight of fame. The platform has long shutdown, but his work there gave him a following of about 3 million, and this carried over into his YouTube career. Logan further diversified by asking his fans to follow him on other social platforms and began promoting himself to them. He is estimated to be worth 19 million dollars, a mark only reached by top income earners on YouTube. Logan has also acted in movies, and this increased his reach and endorsements.

66. Chiara Ferragni

Background

Listed by Forbes among the most powerful fashion influencers, Chiara is a fashion blogger, designer, and influencer. She was born on the 7th of May 1987 and started her fashion blog, *The Blonde Salad,* in 2009, which went big in 2015, pulling the attention of Harvard Business Review. Her blog was seeing a steady stream of about 1 million unique visitors and 12 million views per month, which was unheard of at the time. The Milan native does not have a college degree; she attended Bocconi University to study Law. In 2013, she published an Italian Language book on her blog and modeled for Guess on a campaign that became a huge success. She has also made appearances on television and has tried her hand as a presenter. Chiara's business ventures have brought in nearly $8 million; her blog and shoe line are the major contributors to her income as the modeling comes as an overflow of these two. Her estimated net worth, which is higher than any fashion blogger out there, is pegged at 11 million dollars.

67. Edward Shatverov

Success

An e-commerce guru and all-round internet marketing guy, Edward Shaterov hit the $1 million mark when he was only 18. He is a real estate investor, entrepreneur, and e-commerce expert that owns multi-million-dollar businesses and is regarded to be one of the most influential millionaires on Instagram.

Background

Born in Los Angeles, California, Edward has expressed how being authentic in a sea of conformity is the key to the success he has seen so far; saturation is the order of the day in the market, and carving out a name for yourself is as hard as ever. Estimated to be worth at least 20 million dollars, Edward is continuously pushing the envelope in learning and applying advertising and marketing skills in his business.

68. Chad Rubin

Problem Solver

Chad is the co-founder and CEO of Skubana, a multi-channel software built to help e-commerce brands. He also ranks high on the Amazon Sellers list and has built a $20 million business that is still growing. Chad is a master at sniffing out problems and matching them with solutions; his parents were in the vacuum cleaner business but were hardly making a profit, Chad who was working at Wall Street at the time, was exposed to a myriad of technologies. So, he proposed to his parents that they list out the problems facing the business then find a model that would get the customer's attention online – they were selling out of a retail shop at the time. Chad went on to replicate this model and sell items on different platforms. The one challenge Chad said had plagued him was the invasion of Chinese suppliers offering lower prices and free shipping. Chad's net worth is estimated to be 15 million dollars.

69. Ryan Kaji

Background

Ryan Kaji is the face behind the famous Ryan ToysReview channel on YouTube. The channel was created in 2015 by Ryan's parents when he was 3 years old, for the simple sake of reviewing toys. His first video was of him unboxing and reviewing a Lego train set. This first video now has over 4.8 million views.

Success

Ryan's channel has over 2 billion views, and according to Forbes, Ryan is the highest-earning YouTuber on the block. The channel has over 21.5 million subscribers, and Ryan endorses products and runs review – which has landed the family in trouble with the government over complaints of deceptive advertising – that have netted him a tidy sum. Ryan Kaji's net worth is 16 million dollars.

70. Anthony Morrison

Background

Anthony is a self-taught internet guru and marketer with family at the core of everything he does. He has been a salesman since childhood; he wanted a jacuzzi, but his family could not afford it, so young Anthony, who was

7 at the time, sold candy from door-to-door until he had the money. Growing up in a family that encouraged intellectual curiosity is one of the factors that has kept Anthony curious and in search of solutions to problems.

Hard Times

When financial hardship hit the family, Anthony stepped up and established his first company in his teens. Within a year of creating Cool Blue Performance, which he used to place ads and find spare parts manufacturers, he had already dominated the industry.

Onward

In 2008, he published his first book, The Hidden Millionaire: Twelve Principles to Uncovering the Entrepreneur in You. Then in 2009, he published Advertising Profits from Home. Anthony also partnered with Chicken

Soup for the Soul co-author, Mark Victor Hansen, to create a TV show. Anthony's income mainly comes from affiliate marketing, email marketing, and running Facebook advertisements. He is estimated to be worth 20 million dollars.

71. Evan Fong

Background

As is usual for most YouTube personalities to be most known by their channel name, Evan is popularly known as VanossGaming, a channel dedicated to games and gamers. Evan got started with games like Grand Theft Auto and Call of Duty. His channel grew mainly because of the gaming montage he puts out and his collaboration with other well-known YouTubers.

Diversification

Evan also runs a side hustle where he produces hip hop tracks under a different moniker. His channel has over 22 million subscribers, and he is estimated to be worth 20 million dollars. Between 2018 and 2019, Evan put out more songs and has seen considerable traction.

73. Jake Paul

Background

Jake is a YouTube personality known for his prank-like videos and his influencer program called Team 10. He is the brother of Logan Paul, another YouTube personality that is well-known. Jake has a merchandise side business aside from his YouTube channel and lives on a large piece of property with members of Team

10. He has over 6 million subscribers and is estimated to be worth 19 million dollars at the time of this publication. His videos feature members of Team 10, although some have accused him of non-consensual pranks that endanger them.

21 to 30 Million Dollar Club

74. Evan Luthra

Background

Evan is a whizz-kid that created his first mobile app when he was only 12. The entrepreneur, investor, and visionary first came to limelight when his Instagram account was featured on the Rich Kids of Instagram. The 24-year-old New Delhi born is estimated to be worth 21 million dollars and has been featured on Forbes and other industry media. Through his company El Group, Evan works with entrepreneurs and Fortune 500 companies to create cutting-edge apps. In contrast, his other company Fresh VC gives him the reach to invest in start-ups and push technology towards the future.

75. Neil Patel

Early days

Currently estimated at 30 million dollars, Neil's journey was not at all easy because he was born to a mid-income family and had to manage for most of his formative years. Although surrounding himself with people of vision helped him quickly realize his potentials and the channels that needed his energy.

Success

Neil has spent over a decade working the Internet marketing space, providing solutions, content, motivation, and structure for a lot of individuals and businesses. The 34-year-old UK born digital-marketer founded Crazy Egg and Hello Bar and have previously owned companies that have earned a relatively good income but had to be sold. Neil's YouTube channel is a goldmine for marketers just starting out and intermediates alike for straight edge content and advice.

76. John Crestani

Struggle

Like anyone else, John started as an ordinary guy moving through college and facing the ax of dropping out. He was unsure of life and everything else, so he took a trip to Thailand to think and recharge. While there, he read Tim Ferriss' 4-hour-Workweek, and that was the beginning for him; the book opened his eyes to the possibilities of working a non-conventional job as opposed to the 9-5 everyone was used to doing.

Success

John is an affiliate marketer with a drive to sell products better than the creator. After leaving a job that sucked the life out of him and promising himself never to look back again, John has gone on to become an internationally acclaimed affiliate marketer. He has brought in profit in billions and selling products better than some merchants, which are his slogan and teaching mantra. At the time of this publication, John's net worth is estimated to be around 30 million dollars.

77. Dan Middleton

Background

This UK, born popularly known as DanTDM, started and grew his following to 22 million people with his Minecraft videos on YouTube. Initially, he had named his channel The Diamond Minecraft but later switched to DanTDM for convenience. Dan's Minecraft videos are popular with the younger audience, and his channel is one of the most viewed channels in the UK; he has over 15 billion views on his videos. In 2018, Dan raked in 18.5 million, and his net worth is estimated at 30 million dollars. Dan also published a graphic novel in 2016 that made the New York Times bestseller list for 11 weeks.

78. Ezra Firestone

Struggle

In an interview, Ezra has stated how he used to play poker, and although that lifestyle made him meet degenerates, he took several perspectives that have served him well. Ezra is estimated to be worth 30 million dollars and has said fear is the one limiting factor to success.

Success

Is there money to be made in e-commerce? Your answer would be a resounding yes if you get to meet Ezra or read about all he has managed to do; he made $65 million in sales within 3 years. Ezra is the Co-founder and CEO of Zipify Apps, which was started in 2015 to help productivity and efficiency. He is also the CEO of Smart Marketer Inc., a company created to provide tools to the 21st-century marketers that would help them scale and understand emerging technologies. Even more, he is also the Co-founder and CEO of BOOM BY CINDY JOSEPH LTD, a pro-age cosmetic line for women that was founded in 2010 and has generated a lot of revenue to date. Ezra is a man of many talents, but abides by a mantra, serve the world unselfishly and profit. He has many courses on e-commerce that help the growing entrepreneur to navigate the stream and understand consumer psychology.

79. Mark Fischbach

Background

Known on YouTube as Markiplier, the popular YouTuber born in Hawaii rarely spends time outside of his Los Angeles apartment; creating and editing videos for his channel takes up most of his time. Before fame and YouTube fortune, Mark was a student of Civil Engineering before making the switch to Biomedical Engineering. Finally, he threw in the towel by dropping out to start his channel. Mark has signed multiple endorsement deals and created a clothing line for gamers that have gone on to be a success. Fischbach's estimated net worth is 24 million dollars.

80. Nirav Gandhi

Background

There are people in the Internet space that make a killing yet choose to remain under the radar, Nirav Gandhi is one of these people. Nirav has made almost $200 million at one time while working with a team of 30 and 100 products. A speaker, entrepreneur, and e-commerce expert, Nirav is a specialist at teaching people how to scale their business. And stay on the cutting edge of what is happening; he taught a form of his approach at 2019's iStack Training, which is geared at equipping entrepreneurs that use the Internet to promote sales and understand their market. Nirav is estimated to be worth 30 million dollars.

81. Aimee Song

Background

Aimee is a Californian blogger, Instagram personality, and interior designer that runs a blog called *Song of Style*. In the past, Aimee published her work for free, but as popularity set in, she learned to take those ideas and convert them into money. Her blog has over 25 million views, while her Instagram followers are about 5 million. Her collaboration spanned brands like True Religion and Levi. She was featured on Forbes' 30 under 30 in 2016. Aimee has published a book called Capture Your Style that got on the New York Times bestseller list. Aimee's net worth is estimated to be 21 million dollars.

82. Adrian Morrison

Path

Adrian is the brother of internet guru Anthony Morrison and has spoken about his big brother's influence in his decision to go down this path. Adrian is a master entrepreneur, email marketer, and Facebook advertising guru that has made a lot of money and helped people stand on their own two feet. The brothers have this burning desire to help families and businesses alike to be financially independent.

Background

Born, raised, and still living in Madison, Mississippi, Adrian graduated from the University of Mississippi with degrees in History and Pre-Law; he was still in school when the family came under a dark financial cloud that took Anthony's creativeness to get the family out of that mess. Adrian has made up to $21,000 in a single day and $420,000 in a single month, all from online navigation.

Resolve

He has said that he had decided early on that financial freedom would only come when you are in complete control of your business, and he decided that to be average was not his path in life. Adrian is a smart social media marketer that understands e-commerce, buyer psychology, pay-per-click, and search engine optimization. He had to wear different hats during the heights of his career, and that skills have served him well. Adrian and Anthony started a charity aimed at helping underprivileged kids enjoy Christmas like everyone else, and his net worth is estimated at 24 million dollars.

83. Frank Kern

Background

Frank is an entrepreneur, marketer, and business consultant. Born on the 30th of August 1973, he went to Syracuse University but never did graduate. Frank is one of the leading internet marketers alive and has a huge following online. He is the creator of Behavioral Dynamic Response, an interesting model of selling products directly to the customer that is like direct response marketing; it customizes marketing messages in line with the behavior of the customer.

Early Days

Frank started in 1999 and is famous for using tactics most people would dismiss when it comes to closing deals or selling products. He began as a door-to-door salesman before he had the idea of selling credit card machines online. The wrinkle to this plan was his unfamiliarity with the Internet, and this led him to get an internet marketing course that taught him what he needed to know.

Success

Frank combined this newly acquired knowledge with knowledge gleaned from old seminar recordings that dealt with direct sales and formed a different strategy to accomplish his goals. Frank is estimated to be worth 28 million dollars and is the go-to guy for many online marketers.

84. Felix Arvid Ulf Kjellberg

Background

Popularly known on the Internet by his pseudonym PewDiePie, Felix is a YouTuber with a flair for the dramatic in his videos. He is currently estimated to be worth 30 million dollars, and he has the most subscribed channel on YouTube. The Swedish influencer was born on the 24th of October 1989 and has been interested in art from childhood. Felix is a consumer of video games. He attended Chalmers University of Technology but did not feel he was quite fitted for the system, so he dropped out.

Path

Felix's start was rocky, so he had to make arts on Photoshop for clients so he could get equipment. PewDiePie's reactions and commentaries made him blow up quickly on YouTube. Apart from media deals, PewDiePie also had put out some games and a book that has done well.

31 to 60 Million Dollar Club

85. Tim Burd

Background

Tim is a world-class teacher in the e-commerce space and has taught on subjects ranging from dropshipping, maximizing Facebook ads, and email marketing. He is a serial entrepreneur that has taken many companies and elevated them to 7-figure status; he runs the largest Facebook advertising community and is the co-founder of a digital agency called Agency Y. Tim holds masterminds the world over and is especially suited for high-end advertising.

Path

It took a lot of trial and error for Tim to arrive at this place where he understands the nuts and bolts of Facebook ads and what works when it comes to running a successful campaign and business. He is estimated to be worth 50 million dollars and is one of the most sought-after teachers in e-commerce.

86. Dan Nikas

Struggle

Dan was a homicide detective in Australia but was forced to retire early at 36 due to medical complications. He had been in the force for almost 17 years, having joined when he was 19 and did not know anything other than solving cases and protecting the populace – or so he thought. As it turns out, the skills required to be a good detective translates well in marketing; Dan was used to tracking people that didn't want to be found, but with marketing, clues are all over the Internet, which makes it easy to find people's interests. Dan took the plunge by selling T-shirts on Teespring, a platform specifically designed to handle this niche. The market rewarded his efforts, but everything was getting saturated, and he and his partner, Luuk, needed to find something to make them stand out.

Success

They cracked the code by turning the model on its head, creating a customer avatars and apparels that put the customer first. This took Dan from making $1000 a month to signing a deal with Marvel that put him and his partner at $20 million. Dan's net worth is estimated to be 40 million dollars at the time of this publication.

87. Ryan Morgan

Background

Ryan is a 42-year-old Instagram star that is estimated to be worth 50 million dollars as of 2019's evaluation. He was born in Hawaii and attended the University of Southern California, followed by Loyola Marymount University, from which he graduated in 2011. Ryan's wealth and status primarily come from showcasing his multi-colored hair on Instagram, which is made possible by Co-founder and ex-wife Kristen Leanne's brand Arctic Fox. He and Leanne founded the brand to promote a vegan and cruelty-free alternative to the hair products circulating the sphere. He has more than 100,000 followers on Instagram and a little over 30,000 on YouTube. As any social media influencer would tell you, growing an account and posting content that drives engagement are two difficulties that need to be scaled – this was no different for Ryan – and being different and staying consistent is the cure to his being.

88. RUSSELL BRUNSON

Background

Very few people in the Internet marketing world are unfamiliar with the name Russell Brunson. Russell has built a wall of success and successful people around him. Do you need proof of that? Run a query on Google for ClickFunnels, and you would be pleasantly surprised. Born on the 3rd of March 1980, in Utah, United States, Russell grew from a curious child collecting junk mail and anything that had the smell of money to writing *Dotcom Secrets* and creating a platform geared at promoting businesses. He has sold over 250,000 copies of his books on marketing and general usage of the Internet to your advantage.

Early Days

When he started in the world of online marketing, Russell pedaled a lot of stuff, from software, offering coupons, and consulting services, and selling t-shirts. His approach was punctuated by looking around and trying to find solutions to problems. His first big break came when he secured 1.5 million leads for his diversified portfolio. As for challenges, Brunson faced his fair share of challenges and attributed a large part of his success to Dan Kennedy, who was instrumental in his learning journey.

Breakthrough

Selling potato gun DVDs was his major break into the industry, and this proved that the silliest of ideas had the power to generate income if used rightly. With a net worth of 37 million dollars, this ClickFunnels Co-founder has become one of the biggest names in the Internet marketing space.

89. Nathan Latka

Background

Born on the 3rd of October 1989, in the US, Nathan went to Virginia Tech University and founded Heyo, a company that helps businesses capture email addresses on Facebook. Heyo went on to be a million-dollar company that put Nathan on the list of entrepreneurs that started companies from their dorm rooms; the company was later sold in 2016 after an evaluation that placed it in the 7-8 figure range. He also interviews top performers on a podcast called *The Top* in which he breaks down businesses that are killing it and how they are going about it.

Struggle

Latka has mentioned that building Heyo was tough for him, mainly because he could not code at the time and what he wanted to accomplish needed speed and efficiency. So, what did he do?

Success

He went on YouTube and drank in all the juice available on Facebook Markup Language then built a tool that multiplied his speed. He has also spoken sadly about his job as a cashier at Target; the word job still leaves a bad taste in his mouth. Nathan is currently estimated at 52 million dollars and is still breaking ceilings in the field.

90. Stacey Ferreira

Background

Currently estimated to be worth 55 million dollars, the Scottsdale born entrepreneur and author Co-founded MySocialCloud with her brother while they were in high school.

Path

The idea for the vault app came about after her brother, Scott lost the details in the spreadsheet he was working on. They later sold the app in 2013 to Revolution.com. They moved to San Francisco Bay Area while Ferreira worked on her book 2 Billion Under 20: How Millennials Are Breaking Down Age Barriers and Changing the World, which made it big in the Business Leadership category on Amazon. Stacey went on to Co-found Forge with her brother, an application that tracks and helps hourly workers manage schedules.

91. Lucci Smith

Background

Lucci Smith is an Instagram personality who has achieved fame on the platform via his short dance videos and lip-syncing clips. His Snapchat account also has a rather large following; Smith has achieved online fame quite fast. Lucci is primarily known for his extremely curly locks and is notoriously known for sharing pictures of himself on Instagram. His exotic looks have garnered him more female fans, and the young teen has taken social media by a storm of his own doing. Lucci joined Instagram in 2017, and his first post was a video that got a lot of likes and comments, that helped plant him as an influencer on Instagram. His subsequent post also got a favorable response, and slowly his account began to grow. Born on the 28th of April 2004, in Houston, Texas, Lucci's net worth is estimated to be 55 million dollars.

61 to 80 Million Dollar Club

92. Gallant Dill

Struggle

Gallant Dill is a self-made entrepreneur that dropped out of high school and still made a mark in the world of business. Gallant's first taste of business was at 17 when he realized the gaping hole in most business solutions. So, he went ahead and created a process that could track and render solutions to the problem. This reverse-engineering method made him more than successful at 21, but that did not stop Gallant or make him ease up on his drive and ambition.

Success

He had created a supplement line that had over a million social media followers, which in turn gave him social proof and space in retail stores across the country. Companies approached Gallant to do the same for their brand, which he did and still does so well. The 27-year-old net worth is estimated at 70 million dollars. Austin was born in Texas.

93. Bryan Grey Yambao

Background

Born on the 21st of March 1981, Bryan, also known as Bryanboy on Instagram, is a blogger and socialite from the Philippines. He has a large following on Instagram and is known for his stylish poses, witty captions, and elegant dressing. He has been listed among the 9 hottest celebrities on the web. Before this, Bryan was a web developer and started blogging from his parents' home in Manila. His fans are known for sending in photos of themselves posing in Bryan's signature pose and holding expensive accessory. It has been estimated that his net worth is 67 million dollars.

94. Hershey Hilado

Struggle

Currently estimated at 65 million dollars, the Filipina-Australian entrepreneur did not have it easy growing up; her family sold her off at a point, and she had to find her way to freedom in Australia.

Success

The struggle of being homeless and alone became fodder for Hershey's ambition when she started the commercial fashion brand *Ohmagosh* which serves to connect over 16 countries worldwide. Along with having several other fashion brands under her, Hershey became an advocate for women, so they do not go through the same things she did. She is known for her out-of-the-box approach to problem-solving and establishing dominance in the industry.

95. Jeffree Star

Background

Jeffree is a makeup artist, entrepreneur, musician, and social media personality born on the 15th of November 1985 in Orange County, California.

Struggle

His mother raised him because his father had committed suicide while Star was a child. Star is the founder of the cosmetic company Jeffree Star Cosmetics. He started experimenting with his mother's makeup when he was a child.

Breakthrough

Myspace was Star's first break into the industry as he was promoting his music, life, and fashion design career on the now-defunct social media site. He pursued music for a while at the encouragement of a dear friend but later branched into making videos on YouTube and pushing his cosmetic line. Currently, Jeffree is estimated to be worth 75 million dollars and is one of the most trending people on the Internet.

81 to 200 Million Dollar Club

96. Peter Voogd

Struggle

As a teenager, Peter was frustrated with the state of his finances and swore he would never work another job again. Surprise! Surprise! Peter is a millionaire entrepreneur and author that is setting the bar and helping other entrepreneurs achieve their goals and better their lives.

Success

He got started by selling stuff on eBay and made $91, which was more than he was making at his previous job. Peter learned how to sell and manage properly, then started reaching out to people and multiplied his income. He launched Game Changers Academy, a community built to connect, help, and teach entrepreneurs lessons he learned the hard way. His book *Six Months to Six Figures* has been on the bestseller list on Amazon for a long time. The 31-year-old is estimated to be worth 103 million dollars as of last evaluation.

97. Cameron Herold

Background

Although Cameron's wealth cannot be entirely attributed to the Internet, his use of it is undeniable throughout his career. Fondly called the CEO whisperer, Cameron has a knack for understanding the essence of things and businesses; he already had 14 businesses under his belt by the time he was 18! Cameron is not a stranger to Internet marketing – and marketing in general – he understands the business of growth. He has grown companies from good to great, an example being 1-800-GOT-JUNK from $2 million to $106 million in 6 years.

Struggle

But things were not always rosy for Cameron as a child due to a severe case of ADD, which did not permit him to function properly in a school system. His father took that as an opportunity to teach him to hate work and instead spent time creating businesses. Today, Cameron is worth 106 million dollars, and his books have made the bestsellers list, impacting lives and businesses.

98. Ben Pasternak

Background

Born on the 6th of September 1999, Ben is an Australian entrepreneur with a lot of ambition and drive.

Beginning

He is the co-founder of the social media company Monkey Inc, which was acquired by Holla Inc. in December 2017. While still in high school in Sydney, Ben created two iOS games that went viral, Impossible Rush, and Impossible Dial.

Success

Ben was 15 when he received a round of venture in technology, making him the youngest ever to receive this. Ben was featured in Crain's New York Business Magazine '20 Under 20' and named one of TIME Magazine's Most Influential Teens of 2016. Fortune Magazine has described him as a young innovator who is changing the world. Ben's estimated worth is pegged at 110 million dollars.

99. TIM FERRISS

Background

Known for his books, wit, and motivational videos, Tim Ferriss is an author and entrepreneur that has become a well-known name in the space of personal development and hacking the 21st-century lifestyle. Born in East Hampton, New York, on the 20th of July 1977, Tim attended St. Paul's School in Concord and went on to study West Asian Studies from Princeton University in 2000. He worked in sales for a data storage company while exploring and putting out content on his website.

Path

His career properly kicked off in 2001 with BrainQuicken, an online nutrition supplement that had a large following and solved the imbalance present in the health space. He maintained the website and business for 8 years before selling it to a private equity firm in London. Tim also generated income as an angel investor and advisor to start-ups like DailyBurn, TaskRabbit, Evernote, Lyft, and StumbleUpon. A part of his wealth came from equity stakes in Facebook, Twitter, and Uber, as well as writing and speaking engagements. Currently, Tim's net worth is estimated at 110 million dollars based on recent asset evaluation. He has published books that have made it to the top of the New York Times bestsellers list. The books are 4-hour Workweek and The 4-hour Body.

Obstacles

As for challenges, Tim had to go through a lot of experimentation with balancing work and the desire to hack life; The 4-hour Workweek is a prime example of a lifestyle plan that can only come out of deliberate sousing out of the essential ingredients needed to be successful in this day and age.

100. Gary Vaynerchuk

Background

In the online space, Gary Vee is a legend. His predictions about the direction of social media platforms and content that would be valuable are rarely wrong; he first started this with his family's wine business by leveraging the Internet in a time when few even thought about it. Gary is the king of putting in concentrated work until the results show. Born on the 14th of November 1975 in Bobruisk, Russia, 3 years before his family left Soviet rule to settle in America.

Path

As a child, Gary was involved in various small businesses like running a chain of lemonade stands and selling his neighbors flowers back to them – in an interview; he mentioned making about $3,000 weekly while in middle school. He attended Mount Ida College, Boston, before returning to New Jersey to help run the family business. It was at this time that Gary started making use of what he knew about email marketing to explode the family business by mailing discount codes, coupons, and wine recommendations.

In 2006, Gary started putting out 20-minute videos on his YouTube channel; Wine Library TV grew fast and made Gary a social media personality with something worth hearing. His focus later shifted to digital marketing with VaynerMedia, which serves clients such as Hulu, PepsiCo, the NBA, Shell, and other large corporations. Gary has also authored books that have become coffee table must-read for the budding entrepreneur, as well his podcasts that serve as ginger for the entrepreneur trying to find their footing. Currently, Gary's net worth is estimated at 160 million dollars, and projections see it reaching $200 million by 2020.

Obstacles

Challenges are common in Gary's world, and he expects it: He has spoken at length about not seeing traction early on in his career, but he showed up daily and put in all he had because he believes in the power of work.

Conclusion

In conclusion, I will say this: The opportunities available with the Internet can neither be defined as finite or infinite; it all depends on the perspective of the user, the generation using it, and the iteration it stands on. We have witnessed the growth of the Internet from a terminal-controlled network of computers that accomplished simple tasks to this robust beast that allows us to send large packets of data to rovers out on Mars and carry out business in ways that were previously inconceivable.

Through the years, we have seen and heard stories of people that discovered goldmines from regions that were shunned entirely and disregarded, these same serendipitous-driven discoveries abound on the Internet.

A niche opens, few take the plunge, and fewer still have the strength to stay the course and follow through to the end. As was stated in the introduction to this book, take the stories of these Internet Millionaires as fodder to feed your hustle. Allow their net worth and scaled challenges have a space on your mental and physical vision board. Always have them before you and remember the feeling you got from reading their stories. One more thing, remember why you started. This will serve you well as you journey into the world of Internet ventures.

Cheers to your success!

The Entrepreneur Guy

https://theentrepreneurguy.com/